SCOTTISH TARTANS

by
ALAN BOLD

For such a colourful subject Scottish tartan
has a mysterious past while controversy about
its origins and use continues unabated to
the present day. Only the future seems
unquestionably bright as tartan is firmly
established as an internationally successful
Scottish industry and Highland dress is being
increasingly adopted as a style that combines
both elegance and extravagance.

Tartan samples supplied by The Scotch House
and authenticated by the Scottish Tartans Society.

THE EVOLUTION OF THE TARTAN

The word 'tartan' derived from the words *tiretaine* and *tiritana* which the French and Spanish respectively used to describe a coloured woollen material. In Gaelic the word is *breacan* and was originally applied to an expansive chequered blanket.

In a reference to the Celts in Book 8 of the *Aeneid* Virgil observes: *'Virgatis lucent sagalis'* ('Their cloaks are striped and shining'). Other references to British Celts in speckled and chequered and mottled dress suggest that tartan is an indigenously Celtic phenomenon which was so skilfully developed by the Celts of Scotland that it became the national dress of their country.

It was, however, a slow development and until the 16th century the Scottish Gael dressed in much the same fashion as his Irish counterpart. Nicolay d'Arfeville, Cosmographer to the King of France, wrote of the Scottish Highlanders in 1583: 'They wear, like the Irish, a large and full shirt, coloured with saffron, and over this a garment hanging to the knee, of thick wool, after the manner of a cassock.' Despite this Highland attachment to the saffron shirt, royalty was already using tartan as a decorative addition to courtly clothes for in 1471 James III's treasurer ordered 'Ane halve of blue Tartane to lyne his gowne of cloth of gold . . . Halve ane elne of doble Tartane to lyne riding collars to her lade the Quene.'

By the end of the 16th century the saffron shirt was being replaced, all over the Highlands, by the *breacan feile* or belted plaid. This consisted of six ells (about five yards) of double tartan pleated and fastened round the waist by a belt so that the lower half formed a kilt and the upper half, pinned at the left shoulder with a brooch, hung down as a plaid. It not only left the arms free for work or war but could be reassembled into a blanket if the Highlander had to spend a night out in the open, a circumstance which was by no means unusual.

Portraits show that the belted plaid was the everyday all-weather dress of the ordinary clansmen whereas the Highland nobility only occasionally used it. The chiefs and chieftains and gentry preferred the trews (*triubhas*). Unlike the modern regimental trews, which are really tartan

Right: *A detail from Richard Waitt's portrait of the 15th Chief of Macpherson, c.1700. The Chief is shown in doublet, trews and plaid, which was the form of dress preferred by the Highland nobility.*

Left and left below: *'A Scotch Man' and 'A Highland Man'. This detail from a map of Scotland by John Speed (1552–1629) is one of the first depictions of tartan dress and shows an early stage in the evolution of the belted plaid.*

Below: *This detail of Jeremiah Davison's picture shows a Macdonald boy wearing two different tartans not known today. From such evidence it has been inferred that, prior to the clans' defeat at Culloden, there was no rigid observation of clan or family tartans. This portrait, painted shortly after the Dress Proscription Act of 1747, could be kept with impunity since the boy's father had taken the Hanoverian side during the '45 and the family lived on Skye.*

Right: Portrait detail by J. Michael Wright of Sir Mungo Murray, a 17th-century Highland chieftain. One of the earliest pictures of Highland dress, it shows the belted plaid worn with Restoration doublet and the traditional arms of the Highlander: pistol, dirk, broadsword and long Spanish musket.

trousers, the authentic trews were skintight breeches. They were more appropriate for the horseriding nobility and, because of the considerable skill needed to match the tartan sett in trews, were specially prized.

The Highlanders were well aware that the belted plaid was considered offensive by the Lowland gentry. In 1543 John Elder, a priest, wrote to Henry VIII that 'we of all people can tolerate, suffer and always best with cold . . . going always bare legged and bare foot . . . yet nevertheless . . . when we come to the Court . . . we have as good garments as some of our fellows'. And in 1578 John Lesley, Bishop of Ross, confirmed this when he wrote of the Highlanders: 'If their Princes, or of their nobility, visit the King's Court, they array themselves of a courtly manner, elegantly; when they return to their country, casting off courtly decore, in all haste, they clothe themselves of their country manner.'

Exactly what stage or significance tartan itself had attained at that time is not known. The first tartans were simple checks coloured by the vegetable dyes most easily found in the district. They were made by locals for locals and became district tartans as a rough guide to a Highlander's geographical base. However, a love of colour allied to a practical desire for camouflage made the Highlanders more adventurous and the historian George Buchanan wrote in 1581 that they 'delight in variegated garments, especially stripes, and their favourite colours are purple and red . . . but the majority now in their dress prefer a dark brown, imitating nearly the leaves of the heather, that when lying upon the heath in the day, they may not be discovered by the appearance of their clothes'.

Whether the kilt, as it is now known, had made its own appearance among these clothes is another matter.

The *feile beag* or little kilt is derived from the kilt part of the *breacan feile* or belted plaid. It consisted of six ells of single tartan whose sewn pleats were fastened round the waist with a strap. Today the little kilt is the symbol of Scotland everywhere.

John Taylor's description, from his 1618 observation of the Earl of Mar's hunting party, of Highlanders wearing 'a jerkin

of the same stuffe that their hose is of' suggests the little kilt, as does Thomas Kirk's phrase, in his *Account of Scotland* (1678), about 'a plad tyed about their wastes'. Though these could be confused accounts of the belted plaid it is at least arguable that they refer to the kilt and plaid as separate objects.

It seems likely that the little kilt, 'a servill habit', would have economic attractions for the poorest clansmen who would find the expansive belted plaid too expensive. It is also likely that, as clansmen threw off their belted plaids before battle, the little kilt evolved as a separate item to prevent their indecent exposure. It is, therefore, probably safe to conclude that the belted plaid was a 16th-century improvement on the saffron shirt; that the Highland nobility were the only clansmen who could afford trews for riding and for appearances at the Lowland court; that in the 17th century the little kilt developed as a separate item to be worn with or without a detachable plaid; and that both the belted plaid and the little kilt were in general use up to the Battle of Culloden.

The question of clan tartans is as vexatious a subject as the development of the little kilt. From the extant pictorial evidence it seems clear that, in the era

Left: The official matriculation in 1672 of the Arms of Skene describes the arms being supported 'on the dexter by a Highland man in his proper garb . . . on the sinister by another in a servill habit'. The engraving of the arms, made by Robert Wood between 1695 and 1704 for Nisbet's Heraldic Plates, shows the sinister supporter wearing the little kilt.

Below: Tartan was becoming the sartorial symbol of Scotland. In 1713 the Royal Company of Archers, a Lowland regiment, became the first governmental military body to adopt tartan as part of their uniform. And even after the 1715 Uprising the significance of tartan for Scots was accepted when the Black Watch, raised in 1729, became the first Highland regiment to wear tartan.

Some examples of tartan worn by Scottish regiments are illustrated below. From left to right they are: **The Highland Light Infantry** (City

of Glasgow Regiment) 1929, in MacKenzie tartan, **The Royal Scots Fusiliers** 1933, in an artist's impression of Sutherland tartan, **The Black Watch** (Royal Highlanders) 1936, **The Royal Scots** 1942, in Hunting Stewart tartan, **The Queen's Own Cameron Highlanders** 1927, in an artist's impression of the Cameron of Erracht tartan, **The Cameronians** (Scottish Rifles) 1927, in the Douglas tartan, **The Gordon Highlanders** in the Gordon tartan, and **The King's Own Scottish Borderers** in Leslie tartan.

before Culloden, there were no rigidly observed rules for the wearing of tartans.

On the other hand it is likely that some clans favoured uniformity of colour though it is extremely unlikely that any clans insisted on uniformity of sett.

One of the biggest boosts to the wearing of tartan was the parliamentary Union of 1707 which, in effect, reduced Scotland to the level of a province. Suddenly the tartan became a national symbol of patriotic disapproval of the Union. To Highlanders, who were excluded from the commercial prosperity associated with the Union, the loss of national independence simply confirmed their suspicions of the perfidious *Sassenach* – by which term they meant Lowland Scots as well as the English. And Lowlanders who disapproved of the Union took to wearing such as the Jacobite and Caledonia tartans as badges of their political allegiance.

Disaster for the clans and their distinctive Highland dress came in 1745 in the irresistibly attractive shape of Bonnie Prince Charlie. The persecution that followed the defeat of the clans at Culloden (1746) was not merely a personal campaign by the odious 'Butcher' Cumberland, but part of government policy. They not only disarmed the clans

but denied them their characteristic dress as if they wanted to wipe every feature of Gaelic culture from the face of Scotland.

Thus in 1747 the Act for the 'Abolition and Proscription of the Highland Dress' stated that 'No man or boy within that part of Great Britain called Scotland, other than such as shall be employed as Officers and Soldiers in His Majesty's Forces, shall, on any pretext whatsoever, wear or put on the clothes commonly called Highland clothes (that is to say) the Plaid, Philabeg, or little Kilt, Trowse, Shoulder-belts, or any part whatsoever of what peculiarly belongs to the Highland garb; and that no tartan or party-coloured plaid or stuff shall be used for Great Coats or Upper Coats.'

That, it seemed, was that. Penalties for breaking the law were six months' imprisonment for a first offence and a maximum of seven years' transportation for a second offence. However when the Act was first passed the troops were ordered to 'kill upon the spot any person whom they met dressed in the Highland garb' and this was applied even in the remote areas of the Highlands where the people had neither access to information about Acts of Parliament nor the financial wherewithal to acquire instantly a new and unaccustomed outfit.

THE ART OF BAGPIPE MAKING

It is very unlikely that the Scottish bagpipe originated in Scotland. Two or three centuries ago bagpipes could be found in practically every country in Europe and local varieties are even now played in some remote country districts where old customs have been preserved.

There is fierce competition between bagpipe makers, whose prestige is enhanced by competition prizes won by players of their pipes. The *bag*, made of very soft sheepskin or sealskin, must keep air in and moisture out. Five *stocks*, short heavy wooden tubes, are tied into the bags. The three *drones*, *blowpipe* and *chanter* are pushed firmly into the stocks. The picture above shows the bagpipe maker *hemping* the pipes with yellow hemp, to prevent any air from escaping where two pieces of wood join. The picture on the left shows the Stirling and Bannockburn Caledonian Society tartan.

Women were excluded from the terms of the Act. Wealthy Highland women had long worn elaborate dresses and *arisaid* plaids; clanswomen went bareheaded (and barefoot) before marriage but had a post-marital linen *curac* to cover the head. This style was not, however, encouraged in the Lowlands. In 1631 Edinburgh women were forbidden to wear plaids over their heads and in 1648 the same city ordered prompt punishment – £5 fine and confiscation of the offending garment – for women persisting with their illegal head-covering. And, of course, the Dress Proscription Act did not help. Ramsey of Achtertyre, writing in 1785, said that 'In 1747, when I first knew Edinburgh, nine-tenths of the ladies still wore plaids, especially at church ... so rapidly did the plaid wear out, that when I returned to Edinburgh in 1752 one could hardly see a lady in that piece of dress.'

In fact active persecution of Highland dress virtually stopped when George III came to the throne in 1760. George was fascinated by the romance of the Stuarts and had, in his Scottish Prime Minister Lord Bute, a man well aware of the unnecessary hostility created by the existence of the Dress Proscription Act. In the more relaxed atmosphere the Highland Society of London (founded 1778) appointed a committee to fight for the repeal of the Act. This was achieved in 1782 when the Marquis of Graham, MP (later Duke of Montrose), introduced a repeal Bill which passed unopposed through both Houses of Parliament.

An indication of what this meant to the Highlanders can be gathered from the Gaelic proclamation circulated to announce the repeal. 'Listen, Men!', it began, 'This is bringing before all the Sons of the Gael that the King and Parliament of Britain have for ever abolished the Act against the Highland Dress that came down to the Clans from the beginning of the world to the year 1746. This must bring great joy to

Below: *The Lonach Pipe Band marching to the Lonach Games in Aberdeenshire, followed by representatives of the Forbes and Wallace Clans.*

Right: The creation of contemporary tartans, such as the three on the right was enthusiastically undertaken by Prince Albert. After spending a holiday at Balmoral with the Queen, he bought the 24,000-acre Aberdeenshire estate in 1852. He not only commissioned a new castle but designed a tartan to be the exclusive property of the Royal Family. This Balmoral sett is attractive evidence of Albert's devotion to Scotland, however romantic his conception of Scottish history might have been.

every Highland heart. You are no longer bound down to the unmanly dress of the Lowlander.' However in the 35 years that the ban had been in force many 'Sons of the Gael' had been cleared out of their homes or had emigrated. Highland dress did not immediately revive. It took the showmanship of a great novelist and the willing co-operation of a king to put tartan back on the map of Scotland.

Sir Walter Scott, a celebrated writer and an immensely influential man, remade Scotland in his own image in many ways. He persuaded George IV to visit Scotland and become the first reigning monarch to do so since the time of Charles II. Furthermore he persuaded George to appear in kilt and plaid and let the Highland gentry know that they would be expected to do likewise. George IV revelled in the occasion and this 1822 visit virtually initiated the tartan industry, so great was its impact. The firm of William Wilson & Son of Bannockburn, who had an insignificant list of tartans in 1800, manufactured about 150 at the time of the royal visit. In 1842 the huge catalogue of tartans, *Vestiarium Scoticum*, more impressive for its inventiveness than its authenticity, was published.

Highland gatherings are a feature of Scottish summer life. Clan members, often from far afield, gather to enjoy Scottish games, music and competitions as at the Braemar gathering, 1990.

TARTAN MAKING

The Scottish woollen industry has developed from cottage crafts practised all over Scotland (wool is being dried in Harris, above), to today's highly mechanised operation. Working mills manufacture tartan cloth in the Scottish Borders (see map on p.21).

New tartans are constantly being designed, such as those shown here. The Galloway district tartan was designed in 1950, the Earl of St Andrews tartan, now accepted as a district tartan, in 1930, and the Nova Scotia tartan in 1953.

The symbol of the tartan has expressed a very strong sense of kinship in Scotland since the earliest Scots formed themselves into clans. Until the Battle of Culloden, particular patterns were common to a particular district and were associated with the clans that predominated in each district. 'Every isle differs from each other in their fancy of making Plaids, as in the stripes in breadth and colours. This humour is as different through the mainland of the Highlands in so far that they who have seen those places is able, at the first view of a man's Plaid, to guess the place of his residence' (Martin Martin 1703). But after the '45 and subsequent proscription of the Highland dress, it was probably hatred for the union with England that established the popularity of clan tartan.

The tartan is a symbol of the sense of kinship which has lasted in Scotland ever since the earliest Scots formed themselves into clans. The following list of tartans gives examples of tartans, with clan names and affiliations, the lands with which they are associated, and their slogan. They have been loosely divided into the six areas of Scotland shown on the map on p.28 and should provide an easy reference to tartans and localities. The companion volume to this one, *Scottish Clans*, complements the information given here.

1. Barclay, from the Berkeleys who came to England with William the Conqueror. The Barclays have lands in Kincardineshire and Aberdeenshire.

MOTTO *Aut agere aut mori* Either action or death

2. Farquharson, from Gaelic *MacFhearchair*, meaning 'Son of the very dear one'. Clan Farquharson lands are in Aberdeenshire and Invercauld.

MOTTO *Fide et fortitudine* By fidelity and fortitude

3. Innes, from the town of Innes in Morayshire. Clan Innes have lands in Morayshire.

MOTTO *Be traist* Be faithful

4. Duncan, from Gaelic *Donnachaidh* meaning 'Brown warriors'. Duncan lands are in Atholl and Lundie in Fife. This tartan differs slightly from the usual Duncan tartan which would have wide blue rather than black bands vertically and horizontally.

MOTTO *Disce pati* Learn to suffer

5. Gordon, from the parish of Gordon in Berwickshire. The Gordons went

from the Lowlands to Aberdeenshire in the 14th century. Their lands are in Strathbogie, Deeside and the environs of Aberdeen.

MOTTO *Bydand* Remaining
PIPE MUSIC The Gordon's March

6. Macduff, from Gaelic *Mac-Dubh* meaning 'son of the dark one'. The Macduff lands are in Fife, Lothian, Strathbran and Strathbogie.

MOTTO *Deus juvat* God assists

7. Culloden, This tartan (origin unknown), was worn by a member of Bonnie Prince Charlie's staff during the Battle of Culloden in 1745, after which tartan was proscribed. 'Highly complex tartans were in vogue at the time of the final crash of Jacobite hopes, and here we have one which shows that the Highland love of exuberant colour could express itself with admirable taste.' (D.C. Stewart, *Setts of the Scottish Tartans*).

8. Bruce, named after Robert de Brus, a French knight from Brix. A descendant, King Robert the Bruce, achieved victory over the English at Bannockburn in 1314. The lands of the Bruce clan are in Annandale, Clackmannan and Elgin.

MOTTO *Fuimus* We have been

3.

4.

7.

8.

9. Sinclair, from the French parish of Saint-Clair-sur-Elle in Normandy. The clan's lands are in Midlothian, Orkney and Caithness.

MOTTO Commit thy work to God
PIPE MUSIC The Sinclair's March
Spaidsearachd Mhic nan Cearda

10. MacKenzie, from Gaelic *MacCoinnich*, meaning 'Son of the Fair'. The MacKenzie Clan claims descent from Colin, forefather of the Earls of Ross. Their lands are in Ross and Cromarty and the Isle of Lewis.

MOTTO *Luceo non uro* I shine, not burn
PIPE MUSIC *Caber Féidh*

11. Sutherland, from the district of the same name south of Caithness, which the Normans called *Sudrland*. The clan had associations with the Murrays. Their lands are in Sutherland.

MOTTO *Sans peur* Without fear
PIPE MUSIC The Earl of Sutherland's March

12. Ross, from Ross-shire, *ros* being Gaelic for headland. The clan was originally called Andrias but acquired the earldom of Ross c.1234 and thus a new name. Clan Ross lands are in Rosshire, Ayrshire and Renfrewshire.

MOTTO *Spem successus alit* Success nourishes hope
PIPE MUSIC The Earl of Ross's March

13. Mackay, from Gaelic *MacAoidh*, meaning 'Son of Aodh'. Clan Kay was originally known in Gaelic as Clan Morgain. Their later title of Mackay comes from a chief so named, living at the time of David II. Their lands are in Ross and Sutherland and Argyll.

MOTTO *Manu forti* With a strong hand
PIPE MUSIC Mackay's March

14. Fraser (of Lovat), from the Norman *friselle* or *fresel* from *fraises*, meaning 'strawberry flowers'. Clan Fraser have had associations with Clan Ranald. Their lands were originally in East Lothian but have been more recently in Aberdeenshire.

MOTTO *Je suis prest* I am ready
PIPE MUSIC Lovat's March

15. Keith, from the town of Keith in Banffshire. The lands of Clan Keith are in Caithness, East Lothian. The tartan is usually called Keith and Austin.

MOTTO *Veritas vincit* Truth conquers

16. Gunn (of Kilernan), from Norse 'gunn-arr'. The clan chiefs claimed descent from Gunni, Norse son of Olave the Black, King of Man and the Isles. Clan Gunn have lands in Caithness and Sunderland.

MOTTO *Aut pax aut bellum* Either peace or war
PIPE MUSIC The Gunn's Salute

17. Munro, from Gaelic *Rothach*, meaning 'Man from Ro'. The Munro lands are in Easter Ross and lands north of the Cromarty firth.

MOTTO Dread God
PIPE MUSIC *Bealach na Broige*

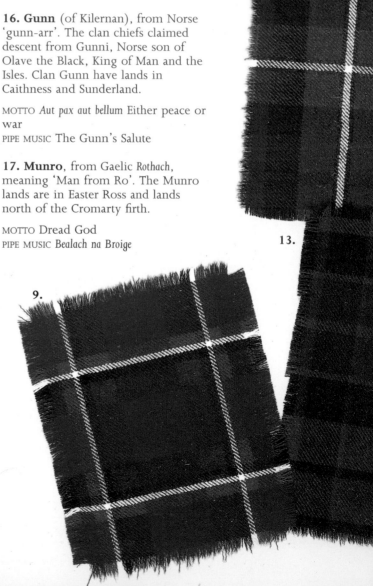

10.

13.

9.

12.

15.

14.

16.

17.

18. Maclean (of Duart), meaning 'Son of Gillean', the 13th-century Gillean of the Battle Axe. Maclean have had associations with the MacLaines of Lochbuie, the MacDougalls of Lorn and the MacDonalds, Lords of the Isles. Their lands are in Morven, Mull, Coll and Tiree.

MOTTO Virtue mine honour
PIPE MUSIC The Maclean's March

19. MacDonald of Clanranald, from MacDonald and Ranald, younger son of John, the first Lord of the Isles. Clanranald lands are in the Northern Isles and North-west Argyll.

MOTTO My hope is constant in thee
PIPE MUSIC Clanranald's March *Spaid searachd Mhic Mhic Ailein*

20. MacNeil(l), meaning 'Son of Niall', the Irish for 'champion'. MacNeill have had associations with the Macleans of Duart and the MacDonalds of Isla. Their lands are in Barra, Gigha, Knapdale and Colonsay.

MOTTO *Vincere vel mori* To conquer or die
PIPE MUSIC MacNeil of Barra's March

21. Grant, from the French *grand*, meaning 'great'. The clan's lands are in Strathspey, Rothiemurchus – around Glen Urquhart, Glen Moriston and Loch Ness.

MOTTO Stand fast
PIPE MUSIC Stand fast Craigellachie

22. MacLeod of MacLeod, from Leod, son of the 13th-century Olave the Black. The MacLeod lands are in Skye, Lewis and Harris.

MOTTO Hold fast
PIPE MUSIC MacLeod's Praise

23. MacDonald, from Gaelic *Domhnull*, meaning 'World Ruler' and Donald, grandson of Somerled, King of the Isles. Clan Donald lands are in the Western Isles.

MOTTO *Per mare per terras* By sea and by land
PIPE MUSIC March of the MacDonalds

24. Macmillan, from Gaelic MacMhaolain, meaning 'Son of the Tonsured One'. Macmillan lands are in Lochaber, Argyll and Galloway. This is Ancient Macmillan tartan.

MOTTO *Miseris succerrere disco* I learn to succour the distressed

25. MacQueen (of Corribrough), from Norse *Sweyne* which probably means 'good going'. MacQueen have had associations with Clan Donald, the Mackintosh and Clan Chattan. Their lands are in Skye, Lewis, Argyll and Lanarkshire.

MOTTO Constant and faithful

26. MacLeod, the branch of the Clan MacLeod descended from Torquil, son of Leod. The lands of this branch are in Lewis, Waternish and Assynt. Some authorities call this tartan MacLeod of Raasay, others MacLeod Dress tartan.

OLD MOTTO *Murus aheneus esto* Be then a wall of brass

20.

21.

23.

24.

25.

26.

27. Caledonia. This tartan was probably designed in the 18th century, or possibly earlier, by an unknown hand. The tartan shown here is a variant; there are other Caledonian tartans which were very popular and have been the choice of a number of pipe bands. Caledonia has been said to be a suitable choice for anyone who wishes to be associated with Scotland but does not wish to wear a tartan associated with other people's names.

28. Graham (of Montrose), from Old English *graeham* meaning greyhome. Clan Graham has origins traceable to the 11th century. In 1782 the Marquis of Graham was responsible for the repeal of the Act of 1747 which prohibited the wearing of Highland dress. Graham lands are in the Barony of Mugdock, north of Glasgow, Loch Katrine in the Trossachs, around Kincardine Castle in Perthshire, and around Dundee and Montrose.

MOTTO *Ne oublie* Do not forget
PIPE MUSIC Killiecrankie

29. Rose, from the Norman family *de Rose*. Their lands are in Strathnairn and Rosshire, and Kilravock Castle is still inhabited by the chief of the clan.

MOTTO Constant and true

30. Cumming, the derivation of which is uncertain. Other forms of this name are Cumin and Comyn. Clan Cumming had lands in Roxburghshire, Buchan, Badenoch and Altyre.

MOTTO Courage

31. Campbell, from Gaelic *cam-beul*, meaning crooked mouth. Clan Campbell lands are in Argyll, Cawdor, Loudon and Breadalbane. This tartan belongs to Campbell of Argyll.

MOTTO *Ne obliviscaris* Forget not
PIPE MUSIC The Campbells are coming *Baile Ionaraora*

32. Robertson, from Robert Riabbhach (Grizzled Robert) Duncanson, 4th chieftain of Clan Donnachaidh, from whom both the Robertsons and the Duncans were descended. Clan Robertson have lands in Struan.

MOTTO *Virtutis gloria merces* Glory is the reward of valour
PIPE MUSIC The Clan Donnachie have arrived *Teachd Chlann Donnachaidh*

33. Murray (of Atholl), from Moray in Morayshire. The clan's lands are in Morayshire and Perthshire.

MOTTO *Tout Prêt* Quite ready
PIPE MUSIC Atholl Highlander

34. Cameron, from Gaelic *Cam-shron*, meaning hook-nose. Clan Cameron lands are in Locheil and Northern Argyll; Achnacarry Castle is still the home of the chief.

MOTTO *Aonaibh ri cheile* Unite
PIPE MUSIC *Piobaireachd Dhonuill Duibh*

35. Erskine, from Sir Henry de Erskine, who owned the Barony of Erskine in the 13th century. The Erskine clan were related by marriage to Robert the Bruce and their lands are in Alloa. This is the black and white version of the tartan of which the same sett is also used by the Ramsay clan.

MOTTO *Je pense plus* I think more

27.

31.

30.

28.

29.

32.

33.

34.

35.

36. Drummond, from Drymen in Stirlingshire. The lands of Clan Drummond are in Perthshire. This tartan is Ancient Drummond, or Drummond of Perth.

MOTTO *Gang warily* Go carefully

37. Hamilton, from the north-of-England town of Hameldone. The Hamilton family are the hereditary Keepers of Holyroodhouse and had lands in Renfrewshire and Arran.

MOTTO Through [*sic*]

38. Montgomerie. Eglinton is the seat of the Montgomeries, later the earls of Eglinton, whose tartan is very similar to this one. The Montgomeries had lands in Eglinton, Ardrossan and Kintyre.

MOTTO *Gardez bien* Look well

39. MacGregor, from Gaelic *MacGrioghair*, meaning 'Son of Gregory'. The clan's motto makes reference to its descent from Grioger, son of King Alpin, in the 8th century. Clan MacGregor lands are on the eastern border of Argyll and the western border of Perthshire.

MOTTO *'Srioghal mo dhrean* Royal is my race
PIPE MUSIC *Ruaig Ghlinne Freoine* Chase of Glen Fruin

40. Lennox district tartan, said to be taken from a copy of a 16th-century portrait of the Countess of Lennox, mother of Henry Darnley, the second husband of Mary Queen of Scots, is one of the oldest recorded. The surname Lennox is usually thought to show relation to Clans Stewart or MacFarlane, any of whom may choose to wear the ancient Lennox tartan.

41. Royal Stewart, from the 12th-century High Steward of Scotland whose descendant Walter, the 6th High Steward, married Marjory, the daughter of Robert the Bruce; from them are descended the Royal House of Stewart. This tartan, always

36.

39.

40.

41.

regarded as belonging to the Royal House of Scotland, is now considered to be the Royal tartan of HM The Queen. The Royal House of Stewart, from whom many noble families have descended, have lands in Renfrewshire, Teviotdale and Lauderdale.

MOTTO *Vivescit vulnere virtus* Courage grows strong at a wound

42. Cunningham (House of Glencairn), from the name of that district, in Ayrshire. The Cunningham family had lands in Kilpatrick, Kilmaurs and Glencairn, although branches of the family are now spread all over Scotland.

43. Wallace, from the term Wallensis which was used to designate the Britons of Strathclyde who were of the same stock as the Welsh. Sir William Wallace was Scotland's greatest patriot, refusing to recognise the sovereignty of Edward I. The Wallaces held lands in Ayrshire and Renfrewshire.

MOTTO *Pro libetarte* For liberty

37.

38.

42.

43.

44.

47.

44. Kerr, possibly from Gaelic *cearr* meaning 'a place of strength' or 'fortress', or a Celtic word meaning strength. Other forms of the name are Ker and Carr. Prominent in Border conflicts, the Kerr family had lands in Roxburghshire.

MOTTO *Sero sed serio* Late but in earnest

45. Douglas, from Gaelic *Dubh-glas*, meaning 'black stream'. The history of the Douglases and of the Scottish throne are closely linked. When King Robert the Bruce was dying he asked Sir James Douglas to 'accomplish my vow' of going to the Holy Land by sending 'my heart there instead of my body'. Black Douglas was killed by the Moors and his bones buried in St Bride's Chapel, Douglas. Clan Douglas had lands in Lanarkshire, Galloway, Dumfriesshire and Angus.

MOTTO *Jamais arrière* Never behind

46. Scott, from the Irish tribe, L.Scoti, which gave its name to Scotland. The Scotts were one of the most powerful border clans and a member of it, Sir Walter Scott, did much to raise the popularity of tartan in the 19th century. One of his most memorable verses must surely be from *The Lay of the Last Minstrel*:

Breathes there a man, with soul so dead,
Who never to himself hath said,
This is my own, my native land!
Whose heart hath ne'er within him burn'd
As home his footsteps he hath turn'd
From wandering on a foreign strand! . . .

Scott lands are in the Borders and Fife.

MOTTO *Amo* I love

47. Ferguson, from the name of Fergus, Prince of Galloway, or King Fergus, founder of the Scottish kingdom that is now Argyll. Clan Ferguson had lands in Argyll, Perthshire, Dumfries, Galloway and the estate of Raith.

MOTTO *Dulcius ex asperis* Sweeter after difficulties

48. Lindsay, from a place-name denoting the 'island of the lime tree' or 'Linden', where Anglo-Norman barons originally held land on the Borders. The Lindsays held lands in the Borders and Angus.

MOTTO *Endure fort* Endure with strength

49. Elliot, possibly from the town of Eliot in Forfarshire. Border clans were fierce and kept the law in their own way. The Elliot clan were one of the largest and fiercest. The Elliots had lands in the Borders.

MOTTO *Fortiter et recte* With strength and right

50. Johnston (or Johnstone), from Old English 'John's *tun*', meaning John's farm. The Johnstons were a warlike Border family remembered in Border song and story. They had lands in the Borders and Aberdeenshire.

MOTTO *Nunquam non paratus* Never unprepared

51. Baird, from Old Scottish *baird* meaning to dress very richly, and from the place name in Lanarkshire. The Bairds had lands in Aberdeenshire.

MOTTO *Dominus fecit* The Lord made

The Plaid itself gives pleasure to the sight,
To see how all its sets imbibe the light;
Forming some way, which even to me lies hid,
White, black, blue, yellow, purple, green, and red.
Let Newton's royal club thro' prisms stare,
To view celestial dyes with curious care,
I'll please myself, nor shall my sight ask aid
Of crystal gimcracks to survey the plaid.

'*Tartana*', Allan Ramsay, 1686–1758

45.

46.

48.

49.

50.

51.

CAIRNGORMS AND EAST COAST

Barclay
Farquharson
Innes
Duncan
Gordon
Macduff
Culloden
Bruce

ISLANDS AND WEST COAST

Maclean
MacDonald of Clanranald
MacNeil
Grant
MacLeod of MacLeod
MacDonald
Macmillan
MacQueen
MacLeod

SOUTHERN HIGHLANDS

Drummond
Hamilton
Montgomerie
MacGregor
Lennox
Royal Stewart
Cunningham
Wallace

NORTHERN SCOTLAND

Sinclair
MacKenzie
Sutherland
Ross
Mackay
Fraser
Keith
Gunn
Munro

CENTRAL HIGHLANDS

Caledonia
Graham
Rose
Cumming
Campbell
Robertson
Murray
Cameron
Erskine

LOWLANDS

Kerr
Douglas
Scott
Ferguson
Lindsay
Elliot
Johnston
Baird

Right: *Blair Castle, owned by the Duke of Atholl, who is still the head of the famous Atholl Highlanders (the only private army in Britain), is open to the public and contains some wonderful Scottish treasures.*

Back cover: *Highland chiefs, the frontispiece of James Logan's* The Scottish Gael, *1831. The origins of the feile beag (little kilt) – a detachable garment as opposed to the kilt part of the breacan feile (belted plaid) – are obscure but evidence suggests it was gradually adopted by the clansmen in the 17th century. Here the kilt and plaid are obviously separate items and the little kilt has sewn-in pleats to demonstrate the sett of the tartan.*

Mary

Joseph

Angel

Donkey

Innkeeper

The Story of
Jesus

Illustrated by Chris Rothero

It's fun to Read Along

Here's what you do –

These pictures are some of the characters and things the story tells about. Let the child to whom you are reading SEE and SAY them.

Then, as you read the story text and come to a picture instead of a word, pause and point to the picture for your listener to SEE and SAY.

You'll be amazed at how quickly children catch on and enjoy participating in the story telling.

ISBN 1-84135-034-6

Copyright © 1992 Award Publications Limited

First published 1992
This edition first published 2000
Reprinted 2002
Published by Award Publications Limited,
1st Floor, 27 Longford Street, London NW1 3DZ
Printed in Malaysia

Palms

Fishes

Jesus

King

Camels

Manger

Wise Men

THE STORY OF JESUS

Once, long ago, a gentle young girl

called  was at home in

Nazareth when an  visited her.

The  's name was Gabriel and

he told  that God had sent

him. "You will have a ," the

 said. "His name will be Jesus,

Son of God."

 was engaged to marry a

carpenter who lived in the same

town. His name was and after

they were married  liked to

watch  at work.  might

be busy making a  or mending

a wooden for a cart but he

always had time for  .

 was soon to have her

 and  was very worried

when he heard that he must take

 to Bethlehem. "We must all

go," he said, "to be counted. The

 commands it."

"I will get some food ready for the

journey,"  said.

When everything was ready they

set out,  seated on a  .

What crowds there were in

Bethlehem! It was growing dark and

 had still not found a room.

He could see how tired  was.

She could scarcely sit upright on the

 .

Then at last  's luck changed.

A kind-hearted offered them

his stable. Thankfully  accepted.

The stable was warm and the

animals there, the big heavy

and the sleepy  , were quiet and

friendly.

That night 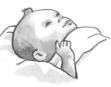 Jesus was born

and  wrapped him in

swaddling clothes.  filled the

 with clean straw so that

could lay him there.

In the morning some  came

to the stable. When they saw the

 in the  , wrapped in

swaddling clothes, they were filled

with joy. "It is just as the

said," one  whispered. "He is

Christ the Lord!"

A bright new in the East

was a sign to three  that a new

 had been born.

The  followed the

through many lands until, at last,

they found the 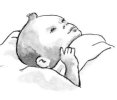 Jesus in

Bethlehem. They bowed low before

him and offered the  the

they had chosen to be fit for a great

. Then they mounted their

 and rode swiftly away back to

their own land.

 did not take his little family

back to Nazareth. Instead he took

the  and his mother to Egypt

where they would be safe from the

wicked Herod.

 Herod had tried to find

the holy child so that he could have

him killed. But  had been

warned in a dream to leave

Bethlehem before Herod's

could discover where they lived.

When the wicked  died they

went back to Nazareth.

 grew up in Nazareth. He

went to school like the other boys

and when he was grown-up he

became a carpenter like  .

Sometimes  talked to the

 on the shore of the Lake of

Galilee.  told them about the

Kingdom of Heaven as they sat by

their mending their  .

Two of the  were brothers.

They wanted very much to try and

be like  . "We will follow you,"

they said. And they left their

and their  and followed him.

One  who loved  was

Peter. He went everywhere with

. Once he joined a great crowd

of people who had come to hear

 speak. The people would not

go home even though they were tired

and hungry.  took a little boy's

supper of two and some small

 and suddenly there was

enough food to feed all the people.

No wonder Peter was astonished!

There was even enough  left

over to fill twelve  .

Sometimes  talked about

going to heaven. He told Peter and

his friends that he would not be with

them for long.

The day came when  said he

must go to Jerusalem and his friends

found a  for him to ride. The

crowds were so happy to see

they waved  in the air and

greeted him with shouts of joy. But

 had enemies in Jerusalem who were plotting to kill him.

That same week  came to the quiet little garden where  was praying. The  took him away and put him in prison. His enemies saw to it that  was sentenced to die on the .

The day  died on the

was a sad day for Peter and his

friends. But  did not leave

them for long. He came down from

heaven to be with them again for a

short time, filling their hearts with

joy and happiness.